THE TAMING

A COMEDY BY
Lauren Gunderson

The Taming (1st ed. - 03.10.15) - thetamingKes
Copyright © 2015 Lauren Gunderson

The Rules in Brief

1) Do NOT perform this Play without obtaining prior permission from Playscripts, and without paying the required royalty.

2) Do NOT photocopy, scan, or otherwise duplicate any part of this book.

3) Do NOT alter the text of the Play, change a character's gender, delete any dialogue, cut any music, or alter any objectionable language, unless explicitly authorized by Playscripts.

4) DO provide the required credit to the author(s) and the required attribution to Playscripts in all programs and promotional literature associated with any performance of this Play.

For more details on these and other rules, see the opposite page.

Copyright Basics

This Play is protected by United States and international copyright law. These laws ensure that authors are rewarded for creating new and vital dramatic work, and protect them against theft and abuse of their work.

A play is a piece of property, fully owned by the author, just like a house or car. You must obtain permission to use this property, and must pay a royalty fee for the privilege—whether or not you charge an admission fee. Playscripts collects these required payments on behalf of the author.

Anyone who violates an author's copyright is liable as a copyright infringer under United States and international law. Playscripts and the author are entitled to institute legal action for any such infringement, which can subject the infringer to actual damages, statutory damages, and attorneys' fees. A court may impose statutory damages of up to \$150,000 for willful copyright infringements. U.S. copyright law also provides for possible criminal sanctions. Visit the website of the U.S. Copyright Office (www.copyright.gov) for more information.

THE BOTTOM LINE: If you break copyright law, you are robbing a playwright and opening yourself to expensive legal action. Follow the rules, and when in doubt, ask us.

Playscripts, Inc.
7 Penn Plaza, Suite 904
New York, NY 10001

toll-free phone: 1-866-NEW-PLAY
email: info@playscripts.com
website: www.playscripts.com

Cast of Characters

All are from Georgia. Actors need not be white.

PATRICIA, aide to Senator Peter Baxter (R-GA), so conservative. 30s.
Also plays JAMES MADISON, 1787

BIANCA, Southern hipster activist, so liberal. 30s.
Also plays INTERN, sweet, Southern good-girl intern.
Also CHARLES PINCKNEY, 1787.

KATHERINE, passionate Southern belle/pageant winner/mastermind. 20s.
Also plays GEORGE and MARTHA WASHINGTON, 1787.
And DOLLEY MADISON (which is just MARTHA with a brown wig)

Voices of:

THE STAGE MANAGER

MISS AMERICA ANNOUNCER

VICTORIA "THE KNIFE" CASTELLIANO

Setting

Now, a nice hotel room in Atlanta, GA.

July 1787, the Constitutional Convention in Philadelphia.

Now, the stage of the Miss Georgia Pageant.

Dramaturgy and Shenanigans HERE:

https://sites.google.com/site/thetamingplay/
and
thetamingplay.tumblr.com

Grammar Note

A character's emotional and vocal emphasis should attempt to build the progression from normal to intense, suggested by the following punctuation and fonts.

> Normal
> Elevated!
> *Intensified!*
> REALLY INTENSE!
> *THE MOST INTENSE!*

Acknowledgments

The Taming was commissioned and premiered by Crowded Fire Theater in San Francisco, California in October 2013, and co-premiered with ArtsWest in Seattle, Washington. The Crowded Fire Theater production was directed by Marissa Wolf and featured the following cast:

KATHERINE . . . . Kathryn Zdan
PATRICIA . . . . Marilee Talkington
BIANCA . . . . Marilet Martinez

THE TAMING
by Lauren Gunderson

Katherine.

(KATHERINE *in a spot*
wearing an American flag dress
and holding a flag or ten.
She's rehearsing for the Miss America Pageant.

She is talking to you, America…)

KATHERINE. Hey y'all!
My name is Katherine Chelsea Hartford from the gorgeous state of Georgia and I'm going to be your next Miss America and make my momma proud. And also Jesus. And George Washington GodBlessAmerica.

(STAGE MANAGER's *voice booms overhead:)*

STAGE MANAGER. Please only do the scripted introduction, Miss Georgia.

KATHERINE. Sorry, this is just so exciting. It's Miss America OhMyGod!

STAGE MANAGER. *(Not thrilled at all:)* Yes we're all thrilled for you, but this is just a sound check. Please continue.

KATHERINE. This is for U…S.A.

(Sung:)

O beautiful for spacious skies,
For amber waves of grain,

> *(As she sings or sing-speaks or whatever is most ridiculous and*
> *sincere…*
> *Her outfit expands or something crazy—lots of flags.)*

STAGE MANAGER. Thank you Miss Georgia, let's move on to—

KATHERINE.
For purple mountain majesties
Above the fruited plain.

STAGE MANAGER. We're don't have time for the whole thing so—

(Maybe streamers or fruit sail out over her head!)

KATHERINE.
> *America! America!*
> *God shed his grace on thee,*

STAGE MANAGER. We have 52 other finalists to get through—

KATHERINE.
> *And crown thy good—*

STAGE MANAGER. I hate my life.

KATHERINE. *with brotherhood—*

> *(Finale! Does this thing light up? That would be awesome.)*

> *From sea to shining—!*

(Drops the smile, out of character:) Is there any way I can I get more flags?

> *(The* STAGE MANAGER *sighs.*
> *Blackout.)*

Patricia.

> (PAT *in a spot,*
> *bitching out an intern in her DC office:)*

PAT. I swear to crispy Christ, Intern, you will get your shit together or you will walk-of-shame yourself across the National Mall, do you understand me?

This isn't a McDonald's. We are getting a major bill through Congress that bears the name of our United States Senator and Future President of Conservative (and the rest of) America.

So when I ask you to proof his memo, I do *not* mean that I want the Senator to *read it*. He doesn't do things like reading. *I do things like reading.* In fact assume that I do *everything* but blink for that man, including and with my bare hands, picking up his heavy Republican feet and walking them into the Oval Office.

*So YOU—little rabbit-breather—*will do nothing that could possibly disrupt the senator or this bill or else the full weight of my political ambition will come crashing down on your sweater set.

Now grab my bag, I'm going to a goddamn pageant.

> *(Blackout.)*

Bianca.

(At the Miss America reception the night before the first day of the competition.
Sounds of rich and/or gorgeous people milling and laughing.)

BIANCA *is getting drunk off sweet cocktails.*
She's judging you.

She is also tweeting the whole time, taking iPhone pics, "reporting"...)

BIANCA. WHOA WHOA WHOA don't you talk to me about the benefits of pageants because that crap is totally crap, ok. Now I am *not* judging you, which I'm really proud of because JESUS you sound Republican, but not only are you supporting a patriarchal institution perpetuating female subjugation through sequins? You seem to be *enjoying it.*

And *that,* Sir, is intolerable.
Oh you're gonna walk away? Nice. Way to engage, buddy.

(She starts tweeting while talking:)

That's what this country needs more of—

(Sending a text:)

—click— *Bad listeners.*

(Sending a text:)

—click.

But you just try to deny the truth. Because the people have the right to know that there are jerks out there—even some *senators in this room*—who would rather DESTROY America than admit that they're WRONG. Which is why some social media soldiers like myself will be forced to take them down in a spectacular and—
dangerously brief fashion. *Tonight.*

(Downs her brightly colored cocktail as…

Spot broadens to include a shocked KATHERINE *and* PAT, *holding a similar brightly colored drink.*

Pause.)

PAT. Excuse me, Very Intense Person. The senator what now?

KATHERINE. YesHi, you said spectacular and dangerously what now?

BIANCA. Patriotism: always online. Click.

(Blackout.)

**(During the blackout and transition
we hear KATHERINE *singing*
"Oh beautiful for spacious skies"
but it starts to sound distorted—tipsy—dreamy...)**

One.

(PAT is asleep in nice hotel room in Atlanta, Georgia.

She is not wearing pants.

She starts awake.)

PAT. *IAmSoAwakeRightNow.*

(Pause.)

Oh god my head. Feels like a cobbler.
Which is no longer comfort food. As I definitely do not know where
I am.

The senator. I must find the senator. He will have some advice on
waking up in strange hotels...with a lack of pants.

Ok. Ok. I remember few and faint details of last night. Sequins. Terrible cocktails. And something that might have been the Archangel
of Flags.

Senator. Must focus on the senator. What if he says what he actually
means on TV? What if CNN asks him to spell something?

Collect your thoughts, Patricia. Life finds a way and so can you.

Blackberry will know what to do. Blackberry? Where are you, Blackberry?

(Can't find her phone...starting to panic:)

THERE IS NO BLACKBERRY—THERE IS ONLY CRISIS—CRISIS
IN AMERICA—OH SWEET JESUS—I NEED MY PHONE—I HAVE
TO BE IN WASHINGTON—I HAVE A BILL—FOR GOD'S SAKE I'M
ONLY BARELY ALIVE IF I CAN'T CALL SOMEONE—

(Looking around for the landline—there is none.)

WHY IS THERE NO PHONE OF ANY SORT IN THIS ROOM?!
Starting to consider potential states of national emergency. Starting
to regret things. Why didn't I run a marathon? Why didn't I try sushi
(I heard some of it's cooked)? If I'd only known I was fated to die

PHONELESS in a hotel I WOULD HAVE RIGHTED THE COURSE OF MY LIFE, I WOULD HAVE—

(*From behind the bed, hidden until now,* **BIANCA** *starts awake.*)

BIANCA. *IAmSoAwakeRightNow.*
Ow. Head. Cobbler.

PAT. *WhoaNow.*

BIANCA. *WhoaNow.*

PAT. Who are you?

BIANCA. Who are *you?*

PAT. Oh my god.

BIANCA. Oh *my* god!

PAT. Ok, I can't tell if you don't speak English or if you're just fucking with me.

BIANCA. I was thinking the same thing. Also it's weird that you have no pants. Also my head hurts.

PAT. WHY DOES YOUR HEAD HURT IN MY ROOM.

BIANCA. IN PART BECAUSE YOU ARE SO LOUD RIGHT NOW.

PAT. WELL MY HEAD HURTS TOO.

BIANCA. THEN STOP YELLING.

(*Pause…*)

PAT. Ok. Ok. What would Condoleezza do?

BIANCA. Uh. What would *Hillary* do?

PAT. Fact finding is the point. A lady, in a bed, in a hotel.

BIANCA. That's how far I've gotten. Also where's my phone?

PAT. I just told you all I know. Now we just need to piece this together. One of us has got to remember something.

BIANCA. I remember Drinking, and Sparkles, and Gorgeous Goddamn People everywhere.

PAT. Definitely at the same party.

BIANCA. I hate Gorgeous Goddamn People Everywhere—where is my *phone?*

PAT. But more to the point of our situation and how soon I need to shower… Did we…? I mean…

BIANCA. I do not remember but I do get pretty gay when I drink.

PAT. DammitDammitDAMMIT.

BIANCA. Well I'm not thrilled either.

PAT. I'M MORE NOT THRILLED TRUST ME. I can't deal with this today, not today.

BIANCA. OkOkOk, tone it down, Red State. *Phone Now Please.*

PAT. I don't have your phone, Blue State.

BIANCA. How do you know I'm a Blue State, Red State?

PAT. Because nothing makes me yell like LIBERALS, now HOW ARE YOU IN MY HOTEL ROOM?

BIANCA. Maybe you're in MY hotel room, NoPants.

PAT. I woke up first, it's my room.

BIANCA. There's some healthy conservative logic.

PAT. I am barely awake, can we not jump straight into partisan crap—

BIANCA. *(Mocking Republicans:)* "If I say it loud enough it must be true."

PAT. *(Mocking Democrats:)* "Ohh if I cry about it, it must be helpful."

BIANCA. *(Mocking Republicans:)* "Ohh if I say 'Main Street' enough people will think I care about the poor."

PAT. *(Mocking Democrats:)* "Ohh if I drain the national defense and pour it into symphonies no one will ever attack us again."

BIANCA. Who *are* you?

PAT. Who are *you?*

BIANCA. *I'm a proud liberal patriot.*

PAT. *That's not a real thing.*

BIANCA. *Neither is a gay Republican.*

PAT. *You'd be surprised.*

BIANCA. *Listen to me.*

PAT. *Listen to me.*

BIANCA and PAT. *We the People is MY People.*

> *(Tense Sexy Partisan Pause…*
> *Tense Sexy Partisan Pause…)*

PAT. Are you sure we didn't…? 'Cause I've been known to enjoy the occasional…

BIANCA. Battle?

PAT. Uh huh.

BIANCA. Uh huh.

(*Tense Sexy Partisan Pause…*)

BIANCA. (*Introducing herself:*) Bianca. Call me Bee.

PAT. Patricia. Speak to me as little as possible.

BIANCA. God, you just wake up mean don't you.

PAT. Oh I sleep mean too.

BIANCA. Well this has been fun but I'm gonna go, and we shall speak of this to no one. I have some statuses to update.

PAT. Some what to what?

BIANCA. Uh. I have Twitter feeds, and hashtags, and MEMES, ok. The internet needs me. *Now where is my phone?*

PAT. Oh god. (*She remembers…*) You're *that* lady.

BIANCA. What lady?

PAT. The *libelous liberal* from last night *threatening my senator.*

BIANCA. Oh you're *that* lady? You work for that hypocrite hawk belching up "family values" but he doesn't seem to *value* the *families* of our smallest mammals.

PAT. Why does it not sound like you're talking about people.

BIANCA. They should be *treated like* people.

PAT. I doubt that, and the senator is a fervent supporter of nature—

BIANCA. For hunting and fracking and *raping our purple mountains' majesty.*

PAT. You have obviously not read our campaign literature.

BIANCA. You have obviously not shared your campaign literature with your uterus.

PAT. MY UTERUS IS CONSERVATIVE.

BIANCA. NOT LAST NIGHT.

PAT. DO YOU KNOW…
(*Trying not to explode:*) how hard I've worked to get where I am? Hard. I have been at this for *decades.* And one day I'll be Chief of Staff or on the Supreme Court literally judging you.
And you, trust-fund beatnik, *you* think you can wake up one day with your shiny progressive outrage and your artful coffee and start

broadcasting your half-thoughts about the government like you even know what it does.

BIANCA. Watch out, Red State.

PAT. SIT DOWN, BLUE STATE.

BIANCA. Not a rocketpop's chance in hell. Because your senator is one "half-thought" away from infamy.

PAT. Whatever you have on the senator is a lie.

BIANCA. Then it's a really elaborate, well-lit lie with explicit audio already formatted for a comfortable viewing experience on all mobile devices. One post and I'm taking you down, though judging by your pants we might've already gone there.

PAT. WOULD YOU JUST GIVE ME PANTS.

BIANCA. I HAVE NOT YOUR PANTS.

PAT. Well I *have not* time for your *blogging,* which I'm sure all two readers of WhinyTimesWhoCares.com will find very compelling, but the rest of us will continue ignoring your miniature crusades and doing real work.

> *(Pause.)*

BIANCA. Million.

PAT. What?

BIANCA. Two *million* readers actually. And they call our action items *tru-sades* because we are fighting the good fight…from our phones. Now I'm sure you and your boss still call it "tweetering," but while you spend all day *almost* making laws that *almost* help people, I'll be getting a few million people to call, think, or donate to anything I want *with one post.*

> *(Pause.)*

PAT. And this is called tweetering?

BIANCA. This is called JUSTICE. I am on a mission, I have a cause, which is that your senator is personally responsible for destroying the second smallest mammal in this great country and this WAR ON RODENTS must end.

PAT. Oh god this is about an animal.

BIANCA. It's not about an animal.

> **PAT.** Wait for it—

BIANCA. It's about *the most important animal in America.*

PAT. There it is.

BIANCA. The North American Giant Pygmy PandaShrew is going to be WIPED OUT because of that bill, and I and the internet will not STAND FOR IT.

PAT. Stand for a PandaWhat? I've never even heard of these things.

BIANCA. Well, somebody put the Georgia Shrew Extermination Project in that bill, so I have become their humble champion.

PAT. Wait. Aren't they the ones spreading herpes to dogs?

BIANCA. *Not all of them.*

PAT. I would like you to take a quick listen to yourself.

BIANCA. I ONLY LISTEN TO MYSELF. So you keep the phone, and your momentary semblance of power. I was about to upgrade. Come at me, destiny!

> *(She tries to open the door to the hallway.
> Locked.)*

BIANCA. Which is locked.

PAT. What?

BIANCA. Destiny seems to be locked.

PAT. I'M LOCKED IN HERE WITH YOU?

> *(PAT tries the door—locked.)*

BIANCA. OkNotFunnySeriouslyLetMeOut.

PAT. It can't be locked, I can't stay in here, open the door.

BIANCA. *I'm trying, it won't open.*

PAT. I have a senator alone at a beauty pageant!

BIANCA. And I have to the right to tweet about that! Find a phone! Call for help!

PAT. THERE ARE NO PHONES, THERE ARE NO EXITS. HELP US, GOD!

BIANCA. HELP US, HIGHER POWER!

PAT. I'M TRAPPED WITH A DEMOCRAT.

BIANCA. I'M TRAPPED WITH A REPUBLICAN.

PAT. RED STATE.

BIANCA. BLUE STATE.

PAT. SEXUAL TENSION.   **BIANCA.** SEXUAL TENSION.

(Discouraged...trapped...they give up...breathy pause.)

BIANCA. All is lost. I die.

PAT. Can we please not get dramatic about it.

BIANCA. I die and I never finish my young adult novel about a wizard who is part bird.

PAT. OhGodKillMeNow.

BIANCA. And my cat might miss me, and my status...will never be updated again.

PAT. Which is worse than death for you hipster people.

BIANCA. HOW AM I ALIVE IF I CAN'T TELL PEOPLE ABOUT IT.

PAT. Ok calm down, you damn hippie. We'll figure this out. Together.

BIANCA. Together?

PAT. Is there another choice? No. And I'm sure...we have *something* in common? You said you have a cat? That's...human.

BIANCA. *(Hopeful:)* You like cats?

    PAT. No.

        BIANCA. YouWannaTalkAboutCats?

        PAT. No.

            BIANCA. I think cats are majestic.

            PAT. I think cats are small witches.

BIANCA. I take it you have a dog then. Named—lemme guess—Reagan?

PAT. *(Lying:)* Uh. No.

BIANCA. And, I'm not judging you but it's a terrier isn't it?

PAT. Reagan is a chocolate lab, ok—that's an American dog.

BIANCA. You do know that Labrador is an island in *Canada*. Land of the free and *home of the cats.*

PAT. *America is a Republican dog lover.*

BIANCA. Oh please, the Founding White Guys were fancy, fussy radicals who gave *birth* to a new nation, which makes them basically *left-leaning cat ladies.*

PAT. Jesus Christ.

BIANCA. Also a Democrat.

PAT. Jesus loves me and I bet your cat *is an asshole.*

BIANCA. Named *Barack Mittens Bader Ginsberg.*

PAT. OH GOD GET ME OUT OF HERE. HELP ME, FLAG ANGEL, HELP ME NOT HIT HER WITH MY ANGRY FIST.

BIANCA. MUST YOU COMMUNICATE ALL THINGS BY YELLING.

PAT. LIBERALS GET YELLED AT. THAT'S THE RULE.

BIANCA. PUT ON SOME PANTS.

PAT. I WISH I COULD.

BIANCA. USE THE SHEET.

PAT. *(Still sounding mad:)* THAT'S A GREAT IDEA.

> *(Wraps the sheet around her. Pause.)*

BIANCA. Wait. A second ago. Did you say "Flag Angel"?

PAT. Yes. You saw Flag Angel too?

BIANCA. With the sequins?

PAT. And the Vaseline on her teeth?

BIANCA. She was perfect.

PAT. She sang to me.

BIANCA. Oh beautiful—

PAT. —for spacious skies! Yes!

BIANCA. We both saw her. Flag Angel is real. She'll let us out— we're saved!

PAT. Flag Angel!

BIANCA. Flag Angel!

PAT and BIANCA. Flag Angel will save us!

> *(A flush from the bathroom.*
>
> KATHERINE, *their Flag Angel, emerges from the bathroom in perfect makeup and pageant outfit.)*

KATHERINE. *HeyY'allHeyY'allHeyY'all,* it's Katherine Chelsea Hartford waking you up to another beautiful day in the greatest nation on earth—now who wants to save America? All right!

BIANCA. Ohmygod.   **PAT.** Ohmygod.

KATHERINE. Not a god but I get that a lot.
Now while your eyes and expectations adjust, a little housekeeping: Here's some aspirin, your pants are being

pressed, there's coffee in the thingy, I have rehearsal in an hour, GoodMorningAndGodBlessAmerica.

PAT. Flag Angel?

KATHERINE. *(Which means "yes":)* Hey, y'all.

BIANCA. You're Flag Angel?

KATHERINE. Hey, y'all.

PAT. But. Why are you *inside* the room? You were supposed to be our way out.

BIANCA. Did they kidnap you too? Oh my god the plot thickens. Who did this to you?

KATHERINE. Who did what to what?

BIANCA. You don't have to protect them, Flag Angel.

KATHERINE. Actually my name is Katherine-

PAT. Flag Angel, you're gonna have to be strong. No matter what Chinese government spy situation they're working for, we'll protect you.

KATHERINE. ThanksSoMuch, but you don't seem to realize that—

BIANCA. I'm sorry you got mixed up in this.

PAT. I'm sure it's my high level security.

BIANCA. Or my renegade activist agenda.

PAT. I am really important.

KATHERINE. Y'all—

BIANCA. Well I'm dangerously important.

KATHERINE. Y'all—

PAT. *(To* KATHERINE:*)* Well, I will not rest until we're out of here and the men responsible for this sabotage are waving at me from behind bars.

KATHERINE. *Y'ALL.*

> *(Breath.)*

This is actually my thing.
So.

> *(She smiles and pageant waves with a soft:)*

Heyyyyyy.

BIANCA. Wait.

PAT. You?

BIANCA. Wait.

PAT. YOU?

KATHERINE. It's me, y'all. I locked you in here. YesIdid.

PAT. WHO ARE YOU, SCARY PERFECT LADY.

KATHERINE. Aren't you sweet. Katherine Chelsea Hartford of Cobb County, current Miss Georgia, competing in the Miss America Competition and Scholarship Award Contest. And I have to say that y'all were making all kinds of assumptions about my ability to sabotage and kidnap based on my gender, ThisIsWhatAFeministLooksLike.

PAT. Not often enough.

BIANCA. *(Offended:)* Hey.

PAT. What is going on, crazy sparkle vixen, why are you doing this?

KATHERINE. First, we are here to change America for the Better. Second, I roofied y'all last night so that we could have this little get-together.
Third, I talk in list form so I can keep my complex plans in order, ok? Ok.

PAT. YOU DRUGGED US?

KATHERINE. Just a bit.

BIANCA. WHY DID YOU DRUG US?

KATHERINE. To form a *more* more perfect union.

PAT. BUT THE SENATOR AND I ARE AGAINST DRUGS.

KATHERINE. Which is why a little went a long way, BlessYourHeart.

BIANCA. The main issue is still GIVE ME MY PHONE, I NEED MY PHONE.

KATHERINE. ThankYouSoMuch, 'PreciateYou, SIT DOWN.
Now. Why why *why* would Miss Georgia roofie a Republican aide and a liberal blogger on the eve of the Miss America Competition? She must have a reason. It must be exciting. I do and it is.

BIANCA. How is this happening?

KATHERINE. Well my daddy taught me devilish charm and my momma taught me *bedazzlement*.

PAT. PLEASE TELL US WHAT YOU WANT, CRAZY SPARKLE VIXEN.

KATHERINE. Why, a restructuring of American Constitutional Government, of course.

(Pause. Repeated exactly the same as before:)

KATHERINE. Why, a restructuring of American Constitutional—

PAT. Ok, if this is a joke from the guys at the Heritage Foundation can we hurry the stripping along.

KATHERINE. I'm not a stripper.

PAT. Not a good one.

BIANCA. I think she's serious.

KATHERINE. As a bald eagle.
When I won Miss Georgia (ThankYouSoMuch) and was on the road to Miss *America* I thought, what does that even mean? And when a horny young man at the Georgia State Fair asked me if I would marry him and what I loved most about America, I told him "BlessYourHeart" and "What I love most about America is its discursive foundations. This country was built for dialogue, reason, compromise, and—" And right then I knew that I had to spend my life fighting for *that* country, not the infighting, name-calling, house-divided country we have now. So I went back to my Constitutional Law degree, which I have y'all and it's very informative, and thought, "Well my goodness, this would work better if we gave this baby a reboot." 'Cause you know Thomas Jefferson himself said we do just that *every generation y'all*—which means we're late by like *two hundred years.* And then last Tuesday I thought "fuck it, is this a Miss AMERICA Competition or what" so I dropped my platform of Sunglasses For Babies (their little eyes!) and switched to Rewriting the Constitution.

(Pause.)

PAT. YOU CAN'T REWRITE THE CONSTITUTION.

KATHERINE. The Founding Fathers did. To replace the Articles of Confederation. 1787, comin' back.

BIANCA. Are you serious?

PAT. YOU CAN'T REWRITE THE CONSTITUTION.

KATHERINE. I can't but *we the people* can. Article Five, which says that two-thirds of the *states* may request a Constitutional Convention. As I mentioned, you know what happened the last time there was a convention to amend our guiding document? We threw it out and wrote a new one.

PAT. Jesus Washington Christ.   **BIANCA.** She just blinded me with government.

KATHERINE. Which is why I need both of you on my team. The time is now.

PAT. *Really? The night before you launch your plan* is the *best* time to drug and take advantage of your team?

KATHERINE. Just drug, BlessYourHeart. One of my talents is amateur pharmacology.

BIANCA. So you need *our* help? As in us *together* on the same team?

PAT. YeahWow that's not gonna happen for a million reasons.

BIANCA. 'Cause we are diametrically opposed on like—everything alive.

KATHERINE. As were the founders of this great nation. You think TJ and BF and puny James Madison and the handsome George Goddamn Washington were besties? They were not. Except GDubbs and Madison, they were totally besties, which is so sweet.
So the reason we are gathered today is simple. To re-design America like the founders intended: through reasonable discourse, ensuring tranquility,and the unbiased fairness that God and George Washington gave us, ThankYouSoMuch.

BIANCA. Ok. Yes. And that all sounds really nice.

PAT. Yeah so does a threesome, but someone always gets hurt.

KATHERINE. *(To* PAT:*)* Not if there's solid leadership, BlessYourHeart.

PAT. OK STOP. I am a really important guy who golfs with really important guys so you have to let me go and set up a normal meeting over lattes and we can work this out.

KATHERINE. One: no dairy on a pageant day. Two: we are doing this tonight. Three: I am not here to imprison you. I am here to convince you that we could be a great a team that can set this country on the path of original intent.

BIANCA. Which was racist, capitalist, misogynistic—

PAT. WHY IS THIS HAPPENING AT A BEAUTY PAGEANT.

KATHERINE. Exposure, SweetMeat. The heartland of America will be tuning in. And since I rocked the prelims like butter on a biscuit (ThankYouSoMuch), I will stand at the apex of this country's held breath ready to enlighten and guide them to a new nation, under—

PAT. SPARKLE-FACE-LADY-PARTS, LISTEN TO ME.
This is a waste of time. No one will take you seriously.

KATHERINE. Why not.

BIANCA. Because of your boobs.

PAT. They are not tuning in to watch your rhetoric, honey.

BIANCA. They're watching your boobs.

PAT. And I'm gonna be real frank with you, because I like you and I want you to grow up to be a good PTA mom or whatever. If anyone tells you they care what you think, they just want to sleep with you.

> (KATHERINE *slams something on something.*
> *She is not fucking around any more.*)

KATHERINE. YOU TWO ARE RELEGATING ME TO NEVER HAVING A PUBLIC THOUGHT WORTH SHARING. Now I am not in charge of my physical nor aesthetic excellence. I don't even *try* to win these goddamn pageants, I just do, which sounds fun, but not when people either hate me, think I'm an idiot, or (as you so brilliantly stated the goddamn obvious) want to OWN ME. But here's a news flash, AngryBirds, I am as smart about this shit as a Founding Father and I bet they took just as long to get dressed as I do.
Do not presume you are better equipped to lead the world than I. Prove it.

PAT. (*Proving it:*) I work for the most powerful senator on the Hill. I got him elected, I know every person and secret passageway (which there are) in the Capitol, and I am owed so many favors by such important people that I could *raise* an army to get my coffee. So when you look at me, see not only the full power of an elected official, but the greater power of an ambitious workaholic with no girlfriend. I am not his aide. I AM HIM.

KATHERINE. Which might be why you're here and he's not.

> (*SexyTensePartisanPause.*)

BIANCA. This room just got real serious.

KATHERINE. And I know about your bill, Miss Patricia. And I know about your political excellence. And I know that you are wasting your talent on that man when it could be better served…in me.

BIANCA. Is it me or is everyone gay.

KATHERINE. Everyone's gay.   **PAT.** It's just you.

PAT. I have survived the Boy's Club that is the Beltway, and not only do they tolerate me now, they *count on me.* So explain to me why the hell I would leave my senator for you?

KATHERINE. Because you believe in the Real America.

So do *you*, Miss Dangerous Journalist, but you are just going about it the wrong, loud way.

BIANCA. I've survived just as much of a Boy's Club as she has. Mine got so bad that after always being assigned these pansy little stories, which were either about makeup or actual pansies, I built my online following into the titanic fist of justice it currently is.

KATHERINE. HushNow, LittleHeads. Here's how it looks from the outside:
(*To* PAT:) You are the Biased, Mud-Stuck Non-Rational Fear-Breeding Government.
(*To* BIANCA:) You are Gossip-Peddling Ego-Fed Obsession with the Miniature Issue.
We represent the triumvirate of the grand and fearful dumbing of America, but we can also beat it.

PAT. And what about you?

BIANCA. Yeah, who are you in this threesome?

PAT. (*To herself:*) Hot in here.

KATHERINE. Why, Spectacle of course.
Entertainment, Glamour, Beauty Myth, The Seen and Not Heard, The Distraction, and The Visual Overwhelm that is stripping us of our own rational analysis until we beat it back with the Fresh Feminist Revolution that is coming down like a Tidal Wave of SELF LOVE, MY FELLOW AMERICANS.

BIANCA. Damn girl.   **PAT.** Damn girl.

KATHERINE. Now I have some proposals I'd like to go over with you, and then I believe, if you work with me, that the new species of American will be born *tonight*.

    (*Pause for awesome.*)

BIANCA. That sounds not as likely as me reputation-bombing a politician I truly hate over an issue that no one else is covering but me. You're not stopping my exclusive.

PAT. HOLD THE PHONE, BLUE STATE.

    KATHERINE. No one's even a little curious?

PAT. You are not gonna trash the senator I've worked so goddamn hard to puppet.

    KATHERINE. You're both super satisfied with your government experience?

BIANCA. Well I am not giving up my scandal for her Whatever-The-Boobs this is.

KATHERINE. Wouldn't change a thing—that'sjustgreat.

BIANCA. The Baxter Bill dies tonight.

PAT. The Baxter Bill is focused on jobs. Actual jobs. *That bill is a goddamned miracle* that will help a lot of Americans and it's not going down because of a *goddamned shrew*.

BIANCA. PANDASHREWS ARE AMERICANS TOO.

KATHERINE. I actually have a section about that.

PAT. YOU ARE A RADICAL LIBERAL LUNATIC—

BIANCA. AND YOU'RE A COLD-HEARTED CONSERVATIVE—

PAT. WHO CAN'T SEE THE COMMON SENSE GOOD—

BIANCA. WHO CAN'T FATHOM BEING KIND FOR KINDNESS' SAKE—

PAT. YOU WOULD RATHER SAVE SOME PANDAMICE INSTEAD OF TAX PAYERS!

BIANCA. IT'S THE PANDA*SHREW* AND THEY WOULD PAY TAXES IF THEY COULD.

KATHERINE. *FOR THE LOVE OF JAMES MADISON CAN I GET A TIME OUT.*

 (Pause.)

PAT. I do love James Madison. Time out accepted.

KATHERINE. I would like to reiterate that y'all are here on MY TERMS, ok? We are all here because tonight is MY SHOW, and I know THE WAY OUT, and if you're not going to jump on MY BANDWAGON I WILL ROLL YOU OVER. I can't believe I have to say this but everyone should be focused on me right now.

BIANCA. Well excuse me for caring about *democracy*. I'll just be over here exercising my right to free press because no politician could outlast the footage I have of your presidential candidate.

PAT. Oh come on, what footage could you possible have?

BIANCA. *The really fucking awesome kind.*
On my phone.
Also, have you seen my phone?

KATHERINE. No one's getting their phones until we change this country.

BIANCA. I AM AN AMERICAN UNDER 30 AND I HAVE A RIGHT TO A PHONE.

KATHERINE. YOUR PHONE IS SLIGHTLY LESS IMPORTANT THAN A HEALTHY GOVERNMENT. NOW TAKE OUT YOUR PENCILS. CHAPTER ONE…

PAT. I. Call. Bullshit.

BIANCA. Excuse me?   **KATHERINE.** Excuse me?

PAT. I think you are full of the shit of a big ol' fiber-loving bull. *(To* KATHERINE:*)* Not you, Miss Georgia, I think you're full of light and song.

KATHERINE. 'PreciateYou.

PAT. *(To* BIANCA:*)* You…are just a grandstanding disrupter who found the only living mammal without a non-profit and concocted some tree-hugging sabotage so that you can have something to live for. My senator does NOT HAVE TIME FOR YOUR AGENDA.

KATHERINE. But my agenda's still on the table, right?

BIANCA. The intern.

PAT. The what?

BIANCA. He had time for the intern.

PAT. He did…whatnow?

BIANCA. Oh yes.

PAT. Oh no.

BIANCA. *Oh* yes.

     KATHERINE. Chapter Four covers interns, so we jump right to—

PAT. An intern. Shit. And you have footage?

BIANCA. So much.

PAT. Audio?

BIANCA. He calls her "porkbelly"—

     KATHERINE. Ooooh.

BIANCA. —on many occasions. And here's the thing about soon-to-be-nominated Republican intern-diddlers… NO ONE LIKES THAT.

PAT. OkOk but how— How do you have this? If she's an intern she's under me and—

BIANCA. In my footage she's under *him*.

PAT. No intern of mine would ever do that—and if she did she would never TELL A BLOGGER.

BIANCA. But she would tell a *sister.*

(Pause.)

PAT. YOUR SISTER IS THE INTERN?

BIANCA. VERY MUCH.

KATHERINE. I see where this is going now.

BIANCA. So this is really a win-win situation—the kind where I win both ways. Because either you kill that bill and save my shrews and I do *not* launch the Tumblr full of very hard-to-explain gifs of the senator mid-pork, or…you test me, commit massive shrewicide, and I unleash the tidal wave of pervy evidence that will make his poor grandchildren wail with horror and confusion, and I become the most powerful guerilla celebrity personality of the year. Either way I fulfill my destiny.
So. Save the shrews. Or…
Will you, nill you
I will bury you.

(Pause.)

PAT. Can I talk to Miss Georgia for a second?

(PAT *and* KATHERINE *secede to a corner.* BIANCA *gloats.)*

KATHERINE. I know what you're thinking: yes this is available in a PDF. And yes I will get a drink with you after the competition.

PAT. Great. Wait. What?

KATHERINE. You don't have to ask.

PAT. I wasn't going to.

KATHERINE. Yeah you were. And I accept. I like your style and covert feminism.

PAT. I'm not a feminist.

KATHERINE. Exactly.

PAT. Kay. Well. Before we get that drink, which I'll be more excited about after this hangover. I need you. To help me. Murder the liberal.

KATHERINE. You're funny.

PAT. Never in my life have I been funny.

KATHERINE. It's funny that you want to murder the blogger and not the senator that would risk all the hard work you've put into him for an intern.

PAT. That's…quite valid.

KATHERINE. ThankYouSoMuch.

BIANCA. See? Yes. Liberal Win!

PAT. YOU DO NOT WIN, I WIN, BECAUSE I KNEW ABOUT THE INTERN.

    (Pause.)

He is not subtle and he calls all of them "porkbelly."

BIANCA. *All* of them?

KATHERINE. Future reference, no woman wants any nickname with "belly."

BIANCA. I knew it.

KATHERINE. Or "pork."

BIANCA. He *is* a terrible person. Oh my god I'm going to have so many new followers. How could you work for that man?

PAT. Because we used to not care about "behavior," we used to care about leadership. And I believe that I did what the founders would've wanted: private oddity shall not infringe upon public good.

KATHERINE. Perfect segue back to my thing: the Founding Fathers believed in—

BIANCA. Yeah I think the visor of your conservative helmet might be down because you can't seem to hear us out here in the real world. *He is a bad guy, which is great for me.* Worse guy, better story, best shot-at-my-own-tv-show.

KATHERINE. Your glee concerns me.

PAT. *The story should be the millions of people who can't afford food.* That's more important than weird sex or sick shrews.

BIANCA. You don't care that your bill will *eliminate an entire species?* That's on *your* head now.

PAT. So is the future of unemployed, hungry families across this country. Giving a shit about one diseased animal is a luxury they *do not have.*

KATHERINE. *(Flipping to another section in her binder:)* Speaking of luxuries that America does not have: the current tax code is—

BIANCA. The intern is in the closet.

PAT. A what.

KATHERINE. A closet?

PAT. A WHAT IS IN A CLOSET.

BIANCA. In my room on the third floor. I thought a visual aid would be helpful. Kill the bill. Save the shrews. And let freedom ring for Intern.

PAT. You are getting scarier and scarier and CAN WE GET THE INTERN OUT OF THE CLOSET?!

BIANCA. She's got Gatorade.

KATHERINE. THAT IS JUST TOO FAR. You tied up your SISTER?

BIANCA. If you're not part of the solution, you're part of the problem.

PAT. You are not some activist anymore, you're an extremist.

KATHERINE. No. You're a FACTION.

PAT. Did you say a faction?

BIANCA. Why, is that a Republican word?

KATHERINE. It is exactly what James Madison was afraid of.

BIANCA. A black president?

KATHERINE. NO.

PAT. Well, probably yeah he was.

KATHERINE. I take James Madison *very seriously*. And he took *factions* very seriously.

BIANCA. Which is what?

PAT. Special interest groups.

KATHERINE. You are a vicious special interest group *of one* unduly influencing the rest of us, and you are making James Madison VERY ANGRY.

PAT. I love that you love James Madison.

KATHERINE. Do you know how long I've been waiting to hear someone say that.

BIANCA. I bet a long time. You are talking about *the* James Madison, right?

PAT. The Father of the Constitution.

KATHERINE. The great American nerd.

PAT. He led the Constitutional Convention in 1787—

KATHERINE. He's the best.

PAT. He *is* the best.

BIANCA. And like really dead.

KATHERINE. But his spirit is alive in us.

> *(A small crisis of heart.)*

PAT. Is it?

KATHERINE. It should be.

PAT. *(She is being sincere:)* Miss Georgia, Miss Liberal. For James Madison, please do not do this to the senator. Not tonight. He deserves to be outed and he will, but I need him unscathed until that bill passes—it's a good bill, I swear to you. I designed that bill to do what my senator couldn't fathom—help people regardless of who they vote for. That's the spirit Madison would want in us. So *after* the bill passes, I will help you however you want. I will champion your PandaThings. But this bill is the culmination of my life's work, and you cannot stop it now. Ok?

> *(Pause. BIANCA starts her Greenpeace freak out.)*

BIANCA. No.

PAT. No?

BIANCA. I mean yes.

PAT. Ok good, I thought that was quite moving.

BIANCA. I mean NO. That bill kills my people.

KATHERINE. Rodents are not people.

BIANCA. But I want to help the poor too.

PAT. Who are *actual* people.

BIANCA. But I've blogged so hard to get the word out about the loss of this great animal. But—oh god—I'm so conflicted—I'm kinda freaking out.

KATHERINE. Breathe, sweetheart.

BIANCA. But I have *causes*. And now my causes are...*competing*. Jobs are good, but shrews are my *thing*. Oh god, will this tyranny of conscience never end!

PAT. Is this "liberal angst"?

> **KATHERINE.** YesMa'amItIs.

BIANCA. SO MANY BELIEFS—HOW DO I GO ON—I love animal rights, but some of my animals *eat the other ones*. And I love women's rights, but some of them are *prettier than I am*. WHAT IF MY ORGANIC PEACHES ARE NOT LOCAL BUT THE LOCAL ONES ARE NOT ORGANIC, AND ALL I WANT TO EAT IS BACON ANYWAY OH GOD.

PAT. Ok seriously you've got to let us out.

KATHERINE. No, ma'am, that is not the plan.

PAT. She's having a Greenpeace Panic Attack, it could last for years, let us out.

KATHERINE. Not until the competition starts, which is soon, and my butt glue is coming off so y'all need to *hush*.

PAT. There will be no hushing—this has gone too far—LET US OUT.

KATHERINE. HELL TO THE GODDAMN NO.

BIANCA. I just want to go home.

KATHERINE. Too damn bad—neither of you are off the hook.

BIANCA. What?

KATHERINE. *I am the hook!*

PAT. Miss Georgia, come on—

KATHERINE. I am an Ambitious American Woman In Evening Wear and I am *not to be fucked with*. So both of you will get on board with my dream of constitutional refurbishment because that's what *James Madison would've wanted*.

(*Pause.*)

BIANCA. I'll get her arms, you get her legs.

(BIANCA *and* PAT *chase* KATHERINE *around the room trying to catch her: We hear a blend of…*)

PAT. Commere, Sparkles. We're getting out of here however we have to. Gimme the key card. God you're fast. This is for America.

KATHERINE. This is not what the founders intended. This is a breach of my right to— Back off. Don't make me exert myself—

BIANCA. Come here you pretty beast—stay still— I will get out of here and ruin that man and take you down to SEQUINED HELL FOR TRAITORS—

(**KATHERINE** *squirts them both in the face with a small water gun.*

They look pissed.

Then they both faint.)

KATHERINE. ThankYouSoMuch.

(*Pause.*)

That was ether.

(**Blackout.**

**Perhaps crashing Americana patriotic music
berates us until we eventually find ourselves...)**

Two.

(PAT—*wearing an 18ᵗʰ century outfit
and wig as* JAMES MADISON.
*She wakes up in a spotlight...in the nether space of history...
at a wooden desk in an airless room
circa Philadelphia 1787...)*

PAT/MADISON. Oh dear.
Oh no this is not right. This is just not... (*Feeling her wig:*) the right
hair...for starters.

(*She notices, or somewhere there appears, a flag with only 13
stars...)*

Or the right flag.

(*To* KATHERINE *and* BIANCA, *whom she's sure are hiding
nearby:)*

Ok.
We might disagree on everything political but we agree on the—you
know—*date*, right? Yeah, this does not smell like the 21ˢᵗ century.

(**KATHERINE,** *as* **GEORGE WASHINGTON,** *enters proudly.)*

KATHERINE/WASHINGTON. WhatUp, Buddy. How the hell are
ya? You feeling loose? Feeling confident? Workin' hard or hardly
working?

PAT/MADISON. Uh—well—I am working very hard at figuring out
what's going on.

KATHERINE/WASHINGTON. I am so with you. God, what a day.

PAT/MADISON. Yes and I'm feeling a little dizzy.

KATHERINE/WASHINGTON. I know, right? I mean will New Hampshire ever shut up?

PAT/MADISON. We're in New Hampshire?

KATHERINE/WASHINGTON. That'd suck, amIRight? Of course I am, I'm George Washington.

PAT/MADISON. You're George WHAT?

KATHERINE/WASHINGTON. Side note: I was thinking about business cards for all us Founders. What do you think if mine just says: "The Monument."

PAT/MADISON. Oh my god.

KATHERINE/WASHINGTON. Not a god, but I get that a lot. Ooh! What if instead of cards we start naming cities after ourselves? Nevermind, we can redistrict later. I am seriously exhausted, buddy. You got any ideas about how to finish this thing?

PAT/MADISON. Still catching up, sorry, the *thing* in question is…?

KATHERINE/WASHINGTON. The Constitution.

PAT/MADISON. The Constitution.

KATHERINE/WASHINGTON. Don't look at me, it's your bright idea.

PAT/MADISON. The Constitution is my idea.

KATHERINE/WASHINGTON. The goddamn switcheroo we're pulling on this young nation. "Nono, we'll just amend the Articles of Confederation, we would never write a whole new thing." Then you show up with one already drafted? You don't look it, but you are deviant. You know I thought you were crazy at first—

    PAT/MADISON. I feel very crazy.

      KATHERINE/WASHINGTON. I know, right?

        PAT/MADISON. I don't think you know like I know.

KATHERINE/WASHINGTON. But the Articles SO needed to suck it. And now they do. Victory! I just wish it were moving along a little faster. *Government,* am I right? Of course I am, I'm George Washington.

PAT/MADISON. And—um—to clarify—*I am…*?

KATHERINE/WASHINGTON. James "The Fed" Madison.

PAT/MADISON. I'm James Madison.

KATHERINE/WASHINGTON. Who else would you be—Hamilton? Hamilton doesn't even want to be Hamilton.

PAT/MADISON. And, um—for context—I think this is 17...?

KATHERINE/WASHINGTON. 87. Hello. James, you're freaking me out here.

PAT/MADISON. *Because I am freaking me out here.*

KATHERINE/WASHINGTON. *Well you better figure your shit out,* 'cause I'm presiding over *your* goddamn convention, like you asked me to, you're welcome. And it's getting HOT AS SHIT in Philadelphia and nobody's opening any windows and WE ARE A SMELLY, LOUD-TALKING BUNCH so we have got to WRAP IT UP, ok?

PAT/MADISON. Yes, Mr. President.

KATHERINE/WASHINGTON. Not president yet, but I appreciate for your future vote, I'mGeorgeWashington.
Now, I've got a guy coming by in a minute who could be the key to this compromise. The Southern states will follow his lead, so you need to seriously dazzle him with your smarts.

PAT/MADISON. But—I'm not really prepared— Why me?

KATHERINE/WASHINGTON. 'Cause you're the nerd, I'm the power, Franklin's the party. Why mess with perfection.

PAT/MADISON. Yeah, but, uh, can't, like, Jefferson do it this time?

KATHERINE/WASHINGTON. *Jefferson?* Is in Paris, the ginger. I swear that guy's always up to something.

PAT/MADISON. Yeah, like declaring *everything,* am I right?

KATHERINE/WASHINGTON. Hell yes you are, the scene stealer.

PAT/MADISON. Wine-maker.

KATHERINE/WASHINGTON. "Employer of servants."

PAT/MADISON. Oooh.

KATHERINE/WASHINGTON. I love the guy but that's a lot of illegitimate children to father. I'm sure history won't notice. So. When Mr. Pinckney gets here compromise with him, ok? Let's Constitute this thing.

PAT/MADISON. Wait. Uh—I just—all the heat—and I'm feeling a little faint—

KATHERINE/WASHINGTON. There's no fainting in America.

PAT/MADISON. But—I mean—can't Hamilton take it over?

KATHERINE/WASHINGTON. HAMILTON? Is a turd. Did he say something to you? GODDAMMIT HAMILTON. That should be on our goddamn flag. I need a drink. MARTHA. WHISKEY. HURRY. James? Quick question.

PAT/MADISON. Yes sir.

KATHERINE/WASHINGTON. Are we doing the right thing here? I mean is this country going to...work?

PAT/MADISON. I believe it will.

KATHERINE/WASHINGTON. Oh good. I don't really have a back-up career. MARTHA?

MARTHA'S VOICE. *(Offstage:)* WHAT.

KATHERINE/WASHINGTON. My sweet petal.

MARTHA'S VOICE. *(Offstage:)* WHAT. GEORGE.

KATHERINE/WASHINGTON. Would you be so kind as to rustle up something perfectly alcoholic for us, darling?

MARTHA'S VOICE. I swear to god, George, when I told you NOT to come to this little convention and NOT to eventually be president of the UNITED STATES OF ASSCHAPS, I did not in fact mean "Gee I can't wait to get your friends a cold one."

KATHERINE/WASHINGTON. Nevermind the drinks honey, go buy yourself a hat.

MARTHA'S VOICE. You bet your HONEST ASS I WILL. A big ol' hat.

> *(Pause.)*

PAT/MADISON. She sounds nice.

KATHERINE/WASHINGTON. Nope.

MARTHA'S VOICE. And Hamilton borrowed your jacket.

KATHERINE/WASHINGTON. GODDAMMIT HAMILTON. Look, we have got to get this thing signed if we're gonna get it ratified if we're gonna have a country...or a vacation.

PAT/MADISON. Yes—great— But General, I'm worried.

KATHERINE/WASHINGTON. Don't worry about the big-state-small-state stuff; we've got a plan for that.

PAT/MADISON. I don't think that's gonna be the issue.

KATHERINE/WASHINGTON. Really? 'Cause we've spent the entire first month nailing down the bicameral shit.

PAT/MADISON. Sir. It's not a big-small issue. It's a North-South issue.

KATHERINE/WASHINGTON. Huh. You think?

PAT/MADISON. Pretty sure. And the potential for powerful factions to—

KATHERINE/WASHINGTON. What is it with you and factions.

PAT/MADISON. They could strangle this country's judgment. Also the Electoral College is maybe not our smartest idea.

KATHERINE/WASHINGTON. *Whaaaaa?* But it's a *college.*

PAT/MADISON. I think somebody thought that up at the *end* of a Friday.

KATHERINE/WASHINGTON. Well I think TJ's right and we need a Bill of Rights.

PAT/MADISON. Oh god, we're gonna *amend* the Constitution before we've even *signed* it?

KATHERINE/WASHINGTON. People gotta know that in this country they get to keep their shit.

PAT/MADISON. You want me to name *all* of their rights? That's gonna take forever.

KATHERINE/WASHINGTON. Naw, just pick a few, be a little vague, kick it to the Supreme Court.

PAT/MADISON. Speech, jury, militia?

KATHERINE/WASHINGTON. What's there to misinterpret.

(WASHINGTON *and* MADISON *high-five.*)

KATHERINE/WASHINGTON. And. I just wanna be real clear that this is my actual hair.

PAT/MADISON. Wow, you *should* be president. Does mine look ok? I feel like this wig's not working.

KATHERINE/WASHINGTON. I cannot tell a lie. (*Totally telling him a lie:*) It looks great.

(BIANCA *enters, as* CHARLES COTESWORTH PINCKNEY, *thinking he's hot shit.*)

BIANCA/PINCKNEY. HeyThere Jerks, trying to steal my freedom today?

KATHERINE/WASHINGTON. (*Does not like* PINCKNEY:) Hello, Charles Cotesworth Pinckney.

BIANCA/PINCKNEY. *(To* WASHINGTON:*)* Hey Dubya. *(To* MAD-ISON:*)* What up nerd.

PAT/MADISON. I'm not a—

KATHERINE/WASHINGTON. *(To* MADISON:*)* YeahYouAre. *(To* PINCKNEY:*)* James, this is Mr. Charles Cotesworth Pinckney from the adorable state of South Carolina.

BIANCA/PINCKNEY. HeyHey.

PAT/MADISON. This guy?

BIANCA/PINCKNEY. HeyHey. Can a founding brother get a beverage? A Southern gentleman doesn't do anything without a beverage.

KATHERINE/WASHINGTON. Let's give it a try.

BIANCA/PINCKNEY. A Southern gentleman does not *try*, he *succeeds*.

PAT/MADISON. Did you say *secedes*? *(To* WASHINGTON:*)* Did he say *secedes*?!

KATHERINE/WASHINGTON. No he didn't. Calm down. We're *all* Southerners here.

BIANCA/PINCKNEY. Relatively. Virginia's *north* of South Carolina.

PAT/MADISON. Uh, Virginia is the heart of the South, sir, we totally out-South you.

BIANCA/PINCKNEY. WE ARE SO SOUTH WE PUT SOUTH IN OUR NAME, THAT'S HOW SOUTH WE ARE.

PAT/MADISON. Why are you yelling?

BIANCA/PINCKNEY. THAT'S HOW SOUTH WE ARE.
General, I refuse to speak with this *Democrat*.

KATHERINE/WASHINGTON. WhoaWhoaWhoa, come on now. James is this country's foremost political mind—

BIANCA/PINCKNEY. NerdyNerdSorry, when do I talk to a *real* man?

> *(Pause. A threat.)*

KATHERINE/WASHINGTON. *(Calling to* MARTHA:*)* MARTHA.

BIANCA/PINCKNEY. *(Scared of* MARTHA:*)* OhWaitNotHer.

KATHERINE/WASHINGTON. *Then sit the hell down.*

> *(*PINCKNEY *and* MADISON *sit.)*

KATHERINE/WASHINGTON. First. You two will get over your-goddamn-selves.
Second. You will put this country's sustainability before your "special interests."
Third. I talk in list form so I can keep my complex plans in order.
Now. I shall lead the battle for whiskey beverages.

PAT/MADISON. Don'tLeaveMeGeorgeNO—

BIANCA/PINCKNEY. Could I order some fries with that? No? Ok.

(WASHINGTON *leaves them. Awkward pause.*)

PAT/MADISON. Mr. Pinckney.

BIANCA/PINCKNEY. Yes, Northern Aggressor.

PAT/MADISON. I am NOT the—*ok.* Look. You don't like me. I get that. So I'm just gonna say it: Slavery's gotta go.

BIANCA/PINCKNEY. I'm going to do the patriotic thing and pretend I didn't hear that.

PAT/MADISON. It's disgusting, no one likes it, it makes us look like animals—

BIANCA/PINCKNEY. You try and feed this nation without it.

PAT/MADISON. Keep your plantations, just pay your workers.

BIANCA/PINCKNEY. What about *your* "workers," Mr. Madison? Are you going to pay yours?

PAT/MADISON. Of course I am!

BIANCA/PINCKNEY. Yeah, well, lemme know when that happens and we can talk about where those wages magically came from. No slavery? No nation.

PAT/MADISON. The northern states are repulsed—

BIANCA/PINCKNEY. Not enough to stop buying our goods.

PAT/MADISON. I know but—

BIANCA/PINCKNEY. Here's what I think. I think we want a government that can survive its first decade.

PAT/MADISON. Yes. Which means we have to compromise. So. What about…the Slave *Trade?* The international *trade of slaves* stops now. No more importing. You can give me that.

BIANCA/PINCKNEY. Can't be done.

PAT/MADISON. Yes it can, stop the ships.

BIANCA/PINCKNEY. I need to restock.

PAT/MADISON. THESE ARE HUMAN BEINGS.

BIANCA/PINCKNEY. FOR WHOM I'VE PAID A LOT. Which means they're my property, which means you are trying to take away my property, which means that you, SIR, are un-American.

PAT/MADISON. I wrote the Constitution!

BIANCA/PINCKNEY. Which is currently *a mess.*

PAT/MADISON. Because YOU insist on slavery!

BIANCA/PINCKNEY. No, it's because *you* insist on *equality,* whatever-the-dumb that means.

PAT/MADISON. *It means exactly what it means!* Or what it *will* mean—I mean, *eventually* it will mean—

BIANCA/PINCKNEY. You say "eventually" a lot for a revolutionary. For this nation to work? It has to get real. Let's not let ideals get in the way of a functioning economy, ok? We're not French.
So lemme be clear. Touch slavery? And I'm leaving.

(*Pause.*)

PAT/MADISON. I'm sorry did you say that you're leaving?

BIANCA/PINCKNEY. Yep. And as goes South Carolina, so goes… other dudes.

PAT/MADISON. So. You'd just go? Just go. Are you serious right now?

BIANCA/PINCKNEY. I need slaves.

PAT/MADISON. And I need GOD to BLESS AMERICA.

BIANCA/PINCKNEY. No slaves, no nation.

PAT/MADISON. *I said keep your slaves,* just keep them *alive* so you don't have to bring over any more! This is basic stuff here. And we believe in the same basic things. We fought for this country—

BIANCA/PINCKNEY. Some of us on an actual battlefield.

PAT/MADISON. I fought in spirit.

BIANCA/PINCKNEY. Yeah well I fought in uniform.

PAT/MADISON. FINE. You're a bigger man than I. Is that what you want to hear?

BIANCA/PINCKNEY. I could hear it without the attitude.

(MADISON *controls his anger:*)

PAT/MADISON. You're right. I apologize. Let's not destroy the Republic in one afternoon. *(Buttering him up:)* It's really not our fault. And I think everyone just wants to help the Southern states unyoke *ourselves* from this terrible burden we've been forced to bear. We inherited this, we don't want this. Let the country take that burden for us. Let us help…us.

(*Pause.*)

BIANCA/PINCKNEY. Ok.
But I want the Electoral College.

PAT/MADISON. The what.

BIANCA/PINCKNEY. Electoral College. I like it. It keeps that whole "democracy" thing under control. Put that in and I'll think about staying.

PAT/MADISON. The Electoral College. Is what you're going to trade for ending slavery.

BIANCA/PINCKNEY. WHOAWHOAWHOA we're not ending it. You said we're not ending it. I'M LEAVING.

PAT/MADISON. NO! NO. We're not ending slavery. Just. Come on. The electoral college is terrible. And this is supposed to be *somewhat* of a democracy, and I'm worried that the college takes direct access away from the public.

BIANCA/PINCKNEY. Exactly.

PAT/MADISON. But the president is supposed to protect the people—

BIANCA/PINCKNEY. States' rights.

PAT/MADISON. This isn't about states' rights!

PAT/MADISON. Free market.

PAT/MADISON. How is this about the free market?

BIANCA/PINCKNEY. Sometimes I just yell those.

PAT/MADISON. This is about the right of the people to elect their commander.

BIANCA/PINCKNEY. Yeah but there is no way that the majority of the electorate can even know who's running for office, much less elect a worthy leader.

PAT/MADISON. You're calling our countrymen idiots.

BIANCA/PINCKNEY. I'm calling the newspapers idiots! They only print gossip. How is an educated white male population supposed to comprehend the subtleties of other educated white males' opinions on important matters for educated white men?

PAT/MADISON. But the principle of the thing is—

BIANCA/PINCKNEY. Principles are useless if the country can't function. Electors solve that. Wham, bam, land of the free, home of the brave!

PAT/MADISON. That's not in the Constitution!

BIANCA/PINCKNEY. National anthem!

PAT/MADISON. Which won't be written for 30 years!

BIANCA/PINCKNEY. *How do you know that?!*

PAT/MADISON. THAT'S UNCLEAR.

> *(Pause. Pause.)*

BIANCA/PINCKNEY. I think you're still upset about slavery.

PAT/MADISON. *I am horrified by it.* I can't stop thinking about it. I employ it, I benefit from it, and I can't get us out from under it and keep this union together. We are not discussing taxes, nor elections, nor even are we discussing democracy—we are ALWAYS DISCUSSING SLAVERY because every goddamn decision comes down to *YOU AND YOUR REFUSAL TO FIND ANY WAY TO RELEASE THIS EVIL THAT IS DROWNING US.*

BIANCA/PINCKNEY. *THAT EVIL IS THE REASON WE HAVE A COUNTRY AT ALL.*

> *(Pause.)*

And the reason I will always win this game of "compromise" is because you need me to.

> *(BIANCA/PINCKNEY is right. Pause.)*

> **(KATHERINE,** *now dressed as* **MARTHA WASHINGTON,** *enters, trying not to punch them for disrupting her nap.)*

KATHERINE/MARTHA. I would just like to say that I hate yelling. And there's been a lot of that going on in here.

BIANCA/PINCKNEY.	**PAT/MADISON.**
Sorry Martha.	Sorry Martha.

KATHERINE/MARTHA. *(To* PAT/MADISON*;)* And you tell Dolley that she can "define the role of the First Lady" over my big hat.

> *(Pause.*
> KATHERINE/MARTHA WASHINGTON *leaves.)*

PAT/MADISON. Mr. Pinckney. I have spent months designing this Constitution, and suffering through a summer locked in an airless room with mostly lawyers. I cannot go through that and enshrine this reprehension.

BIANCA/PINCKNEY. Oh no, I don't want you to put it in there at all. It's already there. Because no matter what you and Jefferson "declared"? We all know who "we the people" really is. It's *us.* Don't you think? Wait, I know what you think. Because we think the same. So why don't you join *Me the People,* and unite these states of America.

PAT/MADISON. No.

BIANCA/PINCKNEY. Slavery is really the fault of the British, they started it. And. Y'know it's in the Bible.

PAT/MADISON. So is eternal damnation.

> **(KATHERINE,** *now dressed as* **DOLLEY MADISON,** *enters. She really wants to be in government but is stuck decorating.)*

KATHERINE/DOLLEY. OhMyGod you *guys, hey it's me Dolley!* What fun you must be having "making laws," and treaties, and— Nono, you don't need my opinion, I'm simply *thrilled* to stand by and interior decorate.

PAT/MADISON. Thank you, honey, but actually we're in the middle of—

KATHERINE/DOLLEY. What do you think we'll want for Christmas at the White House, James? Holly? For Dolley?

PAT/MADISON. Fine.

BIANCA/PINCKNEY. What's a "White House"?

PAT/MADISON. Can we *please* talk about this later, honey?

KATHERINE/DOLLEY. Oh sure yeah, carry on, have fun, I don't even *want* to vote.

BIANCA/PINCKNEY. ThanksForThat.

KATHERINE/DOLLEY. Will the new Constitution need a commemorative cocktail? Because I'm getting very good at *all things temporary.*

> *(KATHERINE/DOLLEY storms/weeps off.)*

PAT/MADISON. I am so sorry.

BIANCA/PINCKNEY. *(Having a thought:)* Huh.

PAT/MADISON. She's very animated.

BIANCA/PINCKNEY. That's actually great.

PAT/MADISON. And pretty much always drunk.

BIANCA/PINCKNEY. *"Temporary"* Slave Trade. Yeah. Perfect. No one can get mad at a "temporary" thing.

PAT/MADISON. Except that you keep air quoting it.

BIANCA/PINCKNEY. We say we'll stop the trade "in a few years." I stay in business, the country stays in business. It even sounds like you wore me down, and—looky there—we have a nation. I can take a special interest in that, how about you?

PAT/MADISON. So… *(Still unconvinced:) Lives* for…

BIANCA/PINCKNEY. For one nation under god indivisible with liberty and justice for…us.

> *(Pause.* BIANCA *extends her hand…*
> PAT *doesn't want to, hates every second of this…but shakes.)*

PAT/MADISON. Agreed. But let's not have our slavery-industrialism become a complex, ok?

BIANCA/PINCKNEY. SureRightTotally.

> *(Exhausted pause. Temporary detente.)*

PAT/MADISON. Charles.

BIANCA/PINCKNEY. Yeah.

PAT/MADISON. I am so…hot.

BIANCA/PINCKNEY. I hear ya, Budsky.

PAT/MADISON. Like. *So* hot.

BIANCA/PINCKNEY. I don't understand why we can't open *one* window.

PAT/MADISON. Just one.

BIANCA/PINCKNEY. A small one.

PAT/MADISON. Air out the wigs at least.

BIANCA/PINCKNEY. Jackson's is made of goat hair.

PAT/MADISON. Yeah we're all really aware of that.

BIANCA/PINCKNEY. You know. We could just show up naked one day—that'd get this thing moving.

PAT/MADISON. Don't say that too loud, Franklin'd do it.

BIANCA/PINCKNEY. America: Never boring.

PAT/MADISON. I move to add that to the flag.

BIANCA/PINCKNEY. So. Since we're friends. Can I tell you what South Carolina thinks we should have as the national animal? We propose pork.

PAT/MADISON. You mean pig?

BIANCA/PINCKNEY. I do not.

PAT/MADISON. We're not putting pork in the Constitution.

BIANCA/PINCKNEY. We are if I say we are.

PAT/MADISON. No we're not.

BIANCA/PINCKNEY. Pork is in.

PAT/MADISON. Pork is out, Charles.

BIANCA/PINCKNEY. PORK OR I'M LEAVING.

PAT/MADISON. YOU CANNOT THREATEN TO LEAVE OVER EVERY DISAGREEMENT AND WE CANNOT PUT THINGS IN THE CONSTITUTION WE THINK ARE AWFUL.

> **BIANCA/PINCKNEY.** Or *delicious.*

PAT/MADISON. *(Starting to think he's made a mistake:)* This must be a document that can be respected for ages.

BIANCA/PINCKNEY. Bacon goes with everything.

PAT/MADISON. This country *will* change, and its government will need to be firm but flexible—

BIANCA/PINCKNEY. Like literally everything.

PAT/MADISON. We need to summon up our longest view of what is good and fair for Future America.

BIANCA/PINCKNEY. Sure but it's not gonna change *that* much.

PAT/MADISON. We could get more states—

> **BIANCA/PINCKNEY.** Don't mess with lucky 13.

PAT/MADISON. What if women become people? Or Italians?

> **BIANCA/PINCKNEY.** *(Like that's crazy talk:)* Or dragons, am I right?

PAT/MADISON. Or what if our muskets shrink and proliferate, and people forget what a militia is, and what if they treat corporations like people, and people like problems, and let zealots who think God is talking to them run for Congress and make actual laws.

BIANCA/PINCKNEY. Yeah that sounds like *not* a thing we would originally intend.

PAT/MADISON. Then we must be explicit. This country will shudder and fall if we are not clear and fair and I take it back. *No slave trade.* We can have no ambiguity in this constitution.

BIANCA/PINCKNEY. Um. Too late, no backsies.

PAT/MADISON. WHAT IS NO BACKSIES.

BIANCA/PINCKNEY. I mean. We shook on it. God saw us.

PAT/MADISON. *I think God will understand.* I am not underwriting a corruption into this country's—

BIANCA/PINCKNEY. *(Calling to* WASHINGTON:*)* GENERAL, I THINK WE FIGURED IT ALL OUT.

PAT. No we did *not!*

BIANCA/PINCKNEY. Huzzah!

PAT/MADISON. There has been no huzzah!

(KATHERINE *enters as* GEORGE WASHINGTON *again.)*

KATHERINE/WASHINGTON. What up, Founders. Did someone say huzzah?

BIANCA/PINCKNEY. General.

PAT/MADISON. General! Listen—

BIANCA/PINCKNEY. We have thusly reached a resolution!

PAT/MADISON. NO, Mr. Pinckney is holding this nation hostage—

BIANCA/PINCKNEY. So here's the deal, we're gonna keep the international slave trade for a few years-ish-kinda.

PAT/MADISON. NO we're not!

BIANCA/PINCKNEY. And in exchange for "phasing out slavery," the South gets the Electoral College!

PAT/MADISON. NO COLLEGE, NO SLAVERY. I am putting my foot down, George—we have to stop this—even Hamilton agrees!

BIANCA/PINCKNEY. GODDAMMIT, HAMILTON.
(To PAT/MADISON:*)* WE SHOOK ON THIS, Madison.
(To KATHERINE/WASHINGTON:*)* We shook, so we'll vote. Let this democracy be a democracy!

PAT/MADISON. *It's not a democracy, it's a fucking republic!*

KATHERINE/WASHINGTON. GENTLEMEN. For the sake of my marriage and my country let me be brief: your version of compromise is the South getting almost everything it wanted to begin with.

PAT/MADISON.	**BIANCA/PINCKNEY.**
I tried to stop it.	That's what the huzzah was for.

KATHERINE/WASHINGTON. And we're sure that this isn't just dropping crap on the future and hoping we don't end up screwing the popular vote and/or bottom out into civil war?

BIANCA/PINCKNEY. Way to buzzkill it, G-Dubbs.

PAT/MADISON. General. Override this. Veto this. We can do better. We can make it *more* perfect.

BIANCA/PINCKNEY. *(A threat to PAT and KATHERINE:)* Do I hear my horse calling? Who's headed south first—me or this deal?

(Pause while WASHINGTON weighs the nation's future.)

KATHERINE/WASHINGTON. *(To PAT:)* Did you shake on it?

PAT/MADISON. Well yes, but—

KATHERINE/WASHINGTON. Ah. No backsies, my friend. It's the law.

PAT/MADISON. But—

KATHERINE/WASHINGTON. Sorry, friend. We vote tomorrow. Bring your fancy pens, you guys. We're signing this thing.

> (KATHERINE/WASHINGTON *leaves.*
> BIANCA/PINCKNEY *is proud.*
> PAT/MADISON *is dismayed, defeated…*
> *Quietly sends a message to Future America.)*

BIANCA/PINCKNEY. Wow. Look at us. We did it. That feels good, doesn't it. Making laws like some law-makers.

PAT/MADISON. *(A prayer to Future America:)* Dear Future America…

BIANCA/PINCKNEY. We compromised the hell out of that.

PAT/MADISON. I think we got some of this right but I know some of you will be disappointed—

BIANCA/PINCKNEY. I think I can start to really *see* our future country taking shape.

PAT/MADISON. Dear Future Country Taking Shape. Fear not. I made sure that you can change the stuff that sucks. Amend. Please. I've got the first ten ready to go. Keep fixing this. Keep going.

BIANCA/PINCKNEY. I can see a country with a love of the outdoors and things pillaged from the outdoors—

PAT/MADISON. Don't fear democracy. Use it. Maybe even call it "the internet"—I don't know.

BIANCA/PINCKNEY. I see a country of business and indoor plumbing. *Indoors? What?—*

PAT/MADISON. The truth is, Future America...we are MAKING THIS UP and we're not GODS and we're going to fail.

BIANCA/PINCKNEY. I see expensive educations, and women in pants, and frothy coffees!

PAT/MADISON. HEAR ME, Future America.

BIANCA/PINCKNEY. It all starts now.

PAT/MADISON. You have to FIX this thing. Keep it alive by keeping it relevant. Help it help *you*. Be good, Future America. Be better than us. Please.

BIANCA/PINCKNEY. Well, Mr. Madison.

PAT/MADISON. PLEASE.

BIANCA/PINCKNEY. It looks like our work is done.

PAT/MADISON. REWRITE THE WHOLE DAMN THING IF YOU WANT TO.

BIANCA/PINCKNEY. And it *also* looks like I...

PAT/MADISON. *(To* PINCKNEY:*)* Got exactly what you wanted, Mr. Pinckney.

BIANCA/PINCKNEY. The American Dream.
Oh say, statesman. Can you see?

PAT/MADISON. *(He fears it.)* I can.

BIANCA/PINCKNEY. By the dawn's early light?

PAT/MADISON. It's like 5pm but—

> *(Suddenly their theme song emerges...*
> *So does*
>
> **KATHERINE** *dressed as a*
> *Symbol of America—whatever that means.*
> *Probably a combo of Miss Georgia and George Washington.*
> *Maybe her sash even reads: Miss Georgia Washington...*
>
> *She sings...or she lip syncs/gestures to the Whitney Houston version of the "Star Spangled Banner."*

BIANCA *celebrates! While* PAT/MADISON *watches, dismayed.*
What will become of us…)

KATHERINE.
What so proudly we hailed at the twilight's last gleaming?
Whose broad stripes and bright stars thru the perilous fight,
O'er the ramparts we watched were so gallantly streaming?
And the rocket's red glare, the bombs bursting in air,
Gave proof through the night that our flag was still there.
Oh, say does that star-spangled banner yet wave
O'er the land of the free—

(Suddenly, at the height of awesome, blackout.

In the darkness, the music gurgles…
We are time traveling, at least it feels like that to PAT.

Then we here a banging, then a rustle,
then a door opening onto…)

Three.

(Lights up on **the same hotel room…**
a few hours later…
empty but for PAT *knocked out asleep.*

Her cellphone is ringing with the "Star Spangled Banner" ringtone.
She wakes up, groggy.)

PAT. *When do I get to wake up in a bed?*

(She recovers from whatever odd position she wakes up in.)

General?
FutureAmerica?

(Sees her phone.)

BLACKBERRY, YOU CAME BACK! Oh thank god.

(PAT answers it but not quick enough.)

PAT. Hello? Hello? Dammit.

(KATHERINE pops up from behind the bed—
Awakening from an ether stupor.)

KATHERINE. Yeah I mighta used too much ether.

PAT. General! General?

KATHERINE. General what? What General?

PAT. You're not General George Washington?

KATHERINE. I definitely used too much ether.

PAT. *Are you or have you ever been Miss Georgia?*

KATHERINE. Hey Y'all.

PAT. Hallelujah, we're back! Ok. We're back, we're modern, and it was all a Musical Social Studies dream.

KATHERINE. GODDAMMIT, SOCIAL STUDIES. Goddammit, stupid dream of a better Stupid America. What is wrong with me? This is a stupid mess, isn't it? It is. DamnDamn*Dammit, America.*

PAT. Whoa. Are you ok, Miss Georgia?

KATHERINE. *(Getting upset:)* I am *not* ok, Miss Patricia. I'm on the floor, I'm tore my hose, and I'm starting to think that I'm a historical revisionist.

PAT. It happens to the best of us.

KATHERINE. I thought this idea would be *uplifting* crazy, but it's just *crazy* crazy. It's not gonna work. I know it's not gonna work. You and Liberal are right. Why would anyone take me seriously, I'm trying to ignite a populist movement to reframe the Constitution *at a pageant.*

PAT. It's a scholarship competition—

KATHERINE. IT'S A PAGEANT. And I'm a beauty queen. And so late for rehearsal they probably think Miss Connecticut finally poisoned me.

PAT. Miss Georgia—

KATHERINE. She laces the hairspray—

PAT. Hey—

KATHERINE. Which is pretty smart.

PAT. Hold on now, Miss Georgia.

KATHERINE. *No, Lady-With-Real-Power-And-Respect. (Having her crisis of confidence:)* America thinks I'm an idiot. And even if she didn't, I don't think America *wants* to get better.

PAT. Yes she does!

KATHERINE. America supports deep fried butter as a snack. She doesn't.

PAT. But James Madison wants her to her to get better. I know he does.

KATHERINE. James Madison would think I'm *crazy*, Patricia.

PAT. *The existence of this entire nation is crazy, Katherine Chelsea Hartford: American Hero.* It was crazy when we fought the best military in the world for our independence. It was crazier when we won. It was craziest when a bunch of rival lawyers agreed on anything much less a Constitution THAT STILL BASICALLY WORKS. Crazy that they put slavery in, crazy that the country held together when they took it out, crazy that it took so goddamn long to get the equality PROMISED TO US by those crazy wig-wearing blowhards. THE ENTIRE HISTORY AND REALITY OF THIS COUNTRY IS INSANE. So the way I see it? The crazier your plan? The better. I'm in.

KATHERINE. You're in?

PAT. Hell yes I am. That's how we love this country. We revive her from the inside out. Like you said.

KATHERINE. But. It'll be hard.

PAT. Nearly impossible, I know. But it makes so much goddamn sense we have to try.

KATHERINE. *(Getting her confidence back:)* Do you wanna maybe see my proposals?

PAT. Like a Founding Father wants property rights. Hit me.

> *(From nowhere* KATHERINE *pulls out a **thick tome of proposals**. There might be two volumes.)*

KATHERINE. Ok. Let's start simply. A cap on terms for Supreme Court Justices.

PAT. No life terms?

KATHERINE. Keeps our Constitutional Interpreters fresh.

PAT. And responsive. I love it. Yes. What else?

KATHERINE. Recalculate the number of Senators—this is way overdue. Underrepresentation is unfair.

PAT. HeyNow. Why not give the big states an extra senator.

KATHERINE. Or two?

PAT. You're welcome, California.

KATHERINE. And Texas!

PAT. Damn right! What about the House?

KATHERINE. Let's double it.

PAT. FUCK YES WE DOUBLE IT!

KATHERINE. Smaller purview.

PAT. Better service.

KATHERINE. Representatives can actually represent their communities!

PAT. OkOk can I say what we're both thinking? Electoral college.

KATHERINE. GONE.

PAT. AND GOOD RIDDANCE.

KATHERINE. And can a girl get a campaign finance amendment.

PAT. And a balanced budget amendment.

KATHERINE. And a Stop-Redistricting-We-Know-You're-Fucking-With-Us amendment.

PAT. Oh my god this could happen. More importantly—

KATHERINE. It *should* happen.

PAT. I can get Baxter on board, a few other key senators, we can rally support, and we can make this country the country Madison wanted.

KATHERINE. We can actually do this. Together.

PAT. I never thought I would un-mockingly say this but: Yes. We can. Now go win us a crown.

> *(They shake on it. They are beaming at each other.*
> *They…are suddenly compelled by each other.*
> *Cute awkward pre-love stuff.*
>
> **KAT** *presents* **PAT's** *missing pants, folded neatly, as a gift.*
>
> KATHERINE *starts getting ready to go throughout the rest of the scene.*
>
> *Adorable. Until a flurry of loud knocks on the room's door shatters the cuteness.*
>
> *Before* PAT *or* KAT *can open the door,* INTERN *enters flustered and furious.)*

INTERN. WHY DIDN'T YOU ANSWER THE PHONE, PATRICIA? WHY DIDN'T YOU SAVE ME?

PAT. Save you?

KATHERINE. I wondered where the liberal went.

INTERN. There's a liberal in here? Ohmygod!

KATHERINE. You're the liberal.

INTERN. What? Ew. What?

PAT. Oh no. She's the intern.

KATHERINE. TWINTERNS?!

INTERN. *What are you talking about?!*

PAT. I remember you now. You're the one who sits in the corner with the Jesus water bottle.

INTERN. It matches the lunchbox. *(Re:* KATHERINE:*)* What is *that?*

KATHERINE. Katherine Chelsea Hartford: American Hero, and you look just like your sister.

INTERN. Except that I'm a beacon of poise and Christian values while she is a member of the "creative class" who LOCKED ME IN A CLOSET. I was stuck there for hours and finally got a hand free and called you TO NO AVAIL and then she came to check on me and then I hit her with my shoe, then I finally had room to get my other hand free, and came here and got scared and found another closet AND IT'S ALL TOO MUCH FOR INTERN!

PAT. Calm down, Intern.

KATHERINE. I'm listening, precious, I just need to get competition-ready.

(KATHERINE *goes to the bathroom to get spruced up.*)

INTERN. A competition?

PAT. Don't worry about it, you're ok now.

INTERN. I WAS *IN THE CLOSET* FOR FAR TOO LONG TO BE OK.

PAT. Totally been there.   **KATHERINE.** Bless Your Heart.

PAT. How on earth did you find us?

INTERN. I just asked the front desk. There is like a whole world happening outside of this room.

KATHERINE. Whaaaat?   **PAT.** Let's just sit down.

INTERN. Not until you tell me why I was in a closet. I had no food, no Instagram. And she took my clothes, Patricia. That cardigan was a silk/cashmere blend that was on sale but no one knows and I want it back.

PAT. Ok we'll get you a new one—

INTERN. IT WAS ON SALE BUT NO ONE KNOWS.

PAT. I said ok, but right now we need to discuss—

INTERN. She always steals my fancy stuff, and she's not even fancy.

PAT. Ok, but right now I need to understand your relationship—

INTERN. Fancy-stealing liberals. I mean really. In a closet? All I had was Jesus and my mental playback of *Real Housewives* episodes. I prayed, I passed out, I dreamed of pulled pork.

PAT. Oh god not pork.

INTERN. The senator loves pulled pork.

    (Leaning back in…)

KATHERINE. How's my butt looking?

INTERN. It looks so good I hate you.

KATHERINE. ThankYouSoMuch.

    (KATHERINE goes back to the bathroom.)

PAT. Ok. Let's just dive in to the real issue. Did you have a relationship with the senator?

INTERN. Well…

PAT. Lemme get to the point here: Is "pulled pork" your code word for sex?

INTERN. Absolutely.

PAT. GODDAMMIT. I told him, one more of these and he's gonna get caught. You can't do this over and over with the same code words. *(To INTERN:)* And you can't tell your liberal relatives about it.

INTERN. I would never—Peter told me to not tell anyone except the senator from Nebraska—I think they have a bet going on.

PAT. OK. You are quitting this affair because he will not leave his wife or return your calls because you are a flavor and this is your week. You are just the next thing in line with heels and an untracked car.

INTERN. He *does* love my mini cooper. Which is also his code word for my—

PAT. SPEAK NOT NO STOP.

KATHERINE. *(Offstage:)* Better than porkbelly.

PAT. Look. I know about your sister, Intern. I know she knows. And that she's a reporter.

INTERN. It's a blog! She's not a "reporter," she's a nobody.

PAT. Nobody with political dirt and wifi stays a nobody.

INTERN. It's not dirt, it's love. He loves me! He told me he loves me.

(This speech brings KATHERINE *out of the bathroom.)*

PAT. He lied! He always lies! To everyone! He uses people and moves on and doesn't want to change this country for the better, he wants it to stay exactly the same so that he can keep promising so that he can keep getting elected. Which is not. Founding. Fatherly.

(Pause. PAT realizes she really despises her boss.)

INTERN. And how does that relate to me?

KATHERINE. Just give her a little space while she hits bottom, ok?

PAT. Oh my god I hate my boss, what have I done with my life.

KATHERINE. One: You're still living. Two: You need to ditch the douchebag because, Three: You deserve better.

INTERN. Hello. What about me? I deserve something.

*(**PAT** has a change of heart.*
She is talking about herself as much as INTERN.*)*

PAT. You deserve better too, Intern. We all do. We the People do. He's not the guy any of us want him to be. So it's time *we* become the guy we want him to be.

KATHERINE. Yes. Yes.

(Pause. Pause.)

INTERN. But the PandaShrews'll be ok right?

PAT. The what?

INTERN. *(Trying not to be caught lying:)* Oh. I mean. My sister mentioned some bill and these very important shrews or something.

PAT. Wait.

INTERN. I mean it sounds like he should just kill that bill anyway and…stuff.

(Pause.)

KATHERINE. Oh wow she is totally not the intern.	**PAT.** Holy shit you're not the intern.

INTERN. What—I am *so* the intern—of course I am.

PAT. You're not the intern!

INTERN. Yes I am! Look at me being the intern. I'm interning! Do you want coffee?

PAT. I knew twins was too plot-friendly, you lying little liar.

INTERN. Then I'd have been a really awesome undercover liar playing you for months and *you* didn't notice till right now.

KATHERINE. Way to play the long con, Liberal.

(INTERN *now admits to being* BIANCA.)

BIANCA. Thank you.

PAT. AHA. YOU ARE THE LIBERAL.

BIANCA. YES—fine—I *am* the Liberal AND THE INTERN. So yes, you got me. But I got your boss. Which means that I am your last chance of saving him by saving shrews. The bill burns or he does.

PAT. You do realize that I don't personally control the Senate.

KATHERINE. Also have you ever heard of entrapment?

PAT. Or DIGNITY? He can sue you. You can go to real people jail for this.

BIANCA. I would be vindicated in the court of public opinion.

PAT. WHICH IS NOT A REAL COURT.

BIANCA. WHATEVER. YOUR SENATOR is MINE. Because you know that the damage will be done the second this goes live. One click and your SENATOR MUST BOW TO ME because I have the proof and I have the power and now I have the RESPECT.

PAT. YOUR face is in those pictures too! How is that going to get you respect?

BIANCA. He liked me in a mask. SAVE MY SHREWS or the story drops now.

PAT. You can't *be* the story and write about it!

BIANCA. WHAT DO YOU THINK SOCIAL MEDIA IS, you RUBE. I TRIED to change the world *your way* with lattes, but...
When in the course of human events it becomes necessary to FUCK SOME SHIT UP TO MAKE YOUR POINT, I DO.

KATHERINE. Don't quote the   **PAT.** I am simply speechless.
Declaration in vain.

BIANCA. Because I am the SCION of our FUCKING AGE and I DO WHAT IT TAKES TO SAVE SMALL MAMMALS FROM LARGER ONES.

PAT. She's still going.   **KATHERINE.** I want to look
                                          away but I can't.

BIANCA. And I may lose the battle... BUT I WILL BECOME SO FAMOUS IN THE PROCESS IT'LL BE JUST AS GOOD AS WINNING THE WAR.

KATHERINE. You. Are James Madison's worst nightmare.

BIANCA. *There are other founding fathers to reference.*
And what I am? Is the most powerful social media lobbyist the NRA has ever seen.

(*Incredulous pause.*)

PAT. The NRA?

BIANCA. Yeah. Obviously.

PAT. The NRA.

BIANCA. Your drop in inflection does not change my answer.

BIANCA.	**PAT.** You. Are working for
The National *Rodent* Associa-	The National Rifle Association?
tion— (*Hearing "rifle":*)	
WaitWhat? *Rifles?* No.	

We're the *other* NRA. The R is for Rodents.
Obviously— That's obvious. Right? Right. Oh god.

KATHERINE. Oh honey. Have you been tweeting for the NRA this whole time?

BIANCA. (*In denial about her terrible mistake:*) THE *OTHER* NRA— *Obviously* my hashtag is not about *guns,* it's about *protecting* the *lives* of the mighty American rodent.

KATHERINE. Is your hashtag #NRAProLife?

BIANCA. (*Admitting her terrible mistake:*) Pro RODENT Life—*Rodents*—Obviously—"Choose Life!"—Oh God.

PAT. Wooow.

KATHERINE. It's trending nationwide.

BIANCA. It is?!

KATHERINE. Because the some oil tycoon is donating ten bucks to the GOP for every retweet.

BIANCA. THE GOP HIJACKED MY HASHTAG?

KATHERINE. And whipped up a fundraiser.

PAT. And this is called *tweetering?*

BIANCA. THE GOP HIJACKED MY PERFECT PRO-PAN-DASHREW-LIFE HASHTAG?! Oh those bastards are gonna pay.

They will pay MIGHTILY and GRUESOMELY. STARTING WITH YOUR SENATOR.

PAT. OH WOULD YOU JUST DO IT ALREADY.
You wanna take down the senator? You want to post those pictures? Do it.

BIANCA. I HAVE MY PHONE, THEY STOLE MY TAG, I WILL DO IT.

PAT. THEN DO IT I SAID. DO IT. NOW.

KATHERINE. What about your bill?

PAT. My bill? Was supposed to be great. But let's be honest, after all the shit I had to do to get it out of committee, it offends no one, accomplishes nothing and thus, OF COURSE IT WILL PASS. It *was* my life's work...but now it makes me sick.
(*To* BIANCA:) So post your post. Because I'm ready for some *real* change and that will not happen working for *him*. It happens when, like our Founders, we innovate and compromise for the greater good.

BIANCA. WHEN HAS THAT EVER WORKED? Compromise caused the Civil War, and the wrong winners on American Idol, and *George Washington should have just nipped this shit in the bud and been a dictator!*

KATHERINE. WhoaWhoaWhoa.   **PAT.** That's not right at all.

BIANCA. The Constitution has never NOT been FUCKED WITH. So no matter how much you rewrite it? It will forever be manipulated, misquoted, or ignored in service of—what was that?—FACTIONS. They run this country. Which *is* what the founders really intended. LEAD WITH GREED, baby.

(*BIANCA wields her phone and with the click of her screen:*)

BIANCA. Click.

(*She launches her tumblr with all the Baxter footage.*)

BIANCA. Expect some amazing emails comin atcha real soon. What do ya think about *that, suckas.*

(*PAT's phone pings with texts already.*
KATHERINE *is quiet and kind.*)

KATHERINE. I think. That you should come work for us.

PAT. *That's* your takeaway?

KATHERINE. (*To* BIANCA:) You're not wrong, Bianca. You're just *doing* it wrong. And one day you'll realize that you could use your impressive skills to tame government, not trash it. So when you're ready for that? Call me.

BIANCA. YeahRight.
(Moved by her shocking faith:) Like I would ever be so moved by your shocking faith in me.
(Back to being mean:) You two lunatics just keep trying to win the hearts and—HA—*minds* of America.
I'll be over here MAKING A DIFFERENCE. ONLINE.
Because you won't always see me...
but I will always be there. Fucking shit up.
Like a *real* American.
(Whispering because the idea is too powerful:) PatriotShrew. Vanish.

*(**BIANCA** exits. They are alone.)*

PAT. I feel like we might be dealing with her for a long time—

(BIANCA enters swiftly.)

BIANCA. Forgot my phone. (BIANCA *grabs her phone:)* Shrew. Vanish. Shut up.

(BIANCA exits, finally. For real.)

KATHERINE. Patricia.

PAT. Yes, Miss Georgia.

KATHERINE. Thanks for believing in me.

PAT. Thanks for giving me my country back.

KATHERINE. You betcha.

PAT. Hey. Win this thing.

KATHERINE. Oh. I will.

(KATHERINE exits.)

(PAT has never felt more free and sure in her life. She dials the senator on her Blackberry, he answers.)

PAT. Senator.
Three things.
One. Check your email.
Two. James Madison really hates you.
Three. I quit.

*(**Swift smash into:**)*

The Stage of the Miss America Competition That Night.

(KATHERINE stands onstage, ready to answer her question.)

MISS AMERICA ANNOUNCER VOICE. And now we arrive to our final finalist for the title of Miss America, Miss Georgia. Your question comes from volatile reality TV star Victoria "The Knife" Castelliano.

VICTORIA "THE KNIFE" CASTELLIANO VOICE. Miss Georgia. What advice do you think the Founding Fathers would have to give our current Congress?

KATHERINE. It depends on who you asked, but I believe that James Madison would tell our senators that:
We the People are thy lord, thy life, thy keeper.
I am ashamed that Congressmen are so simple
To offer war where they should kneel for peace;
Or seek for rule, supremacy and sway,
When they are bound to serve, love and obey...

(As though continuing the speech in iambic pentameter:)

The Constitution which needs overhaul,
ThankYouSoMuch, and I AppreciateY'all.

> *(Pomp!*
> *Ceremony!*
> *Miss America theme music!*
> *She won! A crown? Yeah!*
>
> *Then a crashing blackout except for a tight spot on* KATHERINE. *Calm, poised, presidential...*
>
> **Then from the future...)**

The Future White House.

(PAT *walks in as* **KATHERINE's** *Chief of Staff.)*

PAT. Excuse me, Madam President?

PRESIDENT KATHERINE CHELSEA HARTFORD. Yes, Patricia, my Chief of Staff.

PAT. Madam, I have the first draft of your opening remarks for the Constitutional Convention on Monday. I thought you'd like to look it over and work some changes with me. I think it's going to be great.

> **(BIANCA** *enters as her absolutely professional Press Secretary.)*

BIANCA. Madam President. I'm so sorry to interrupt.

PRESIDENT KATHERINE CHELSEA HARTFORD. You're not interrupting, Bianca, my Press Secretary.

BIANCA. I just wanted to hear the new speech to prep for the convention.

PRESIDENT KATHERINE CHELSEA HARTFORD. Of course, come on in.

BIANCA. Thank you, Madam President.

PRESIDENT KATHERINE CHELSEA HARTFORD. Ladies. I think James would be proud of us. And I just want start today by saying… *(She really means this:)*
ThankY'all. SoMuch.
And I 'preciateY'all.
And who needs a Dance Break For America, AmIRight? Of CourseIAm
I'mThePresident.

> *(Awesome dance music — maybe a pop version of*
> *"Hail to The Chief"? — blares and they rock out real quick before…*
> KATHERINE *cuts off the music.)*

PRESIDENT KATHERINE CHELSEA HARTFORD. *(Totally presidential again:)* But seriously I'm the President. Let's get to work.

(Blackout.)

End of Play